Divine Spark
Sumanth Batchu
Sri Ramaraksha Stotra
Spardha 2012

Christ and Oriental Ideals

Christ and Oriental Ideals

BY
SWAMI PARAMANANDA

Fifth Edition

Published by
THE VEDANTA CENTRE, COHASSET, MASS.

ANANDA ASHRAMA
La Crescenta, California

CONTENTS

PART II

ORIENTAL IDEALS (Selections)

WHO IS A CHRISTIAN?

"Shall we say, then, that there were no Christians before Christ, and that there are no Christians outside of what we call Christendom?" Augustine was wiser than that. He refers somewhere to that which has always been in the world from the beginning, and which, in these latter days, we have come to call Christian. So Augustine, the old Church Father and theologian, recognized that what we regarded as important and essential in Christianity was older than what had gone by that name ... The ideal man is the man who loves, and the man who knows how to apply his love power and impetus in such a way as to help, save, transform, develop and glorify mankind ... and I think the man who embodies these three things is a Christian, whatever else he believes."

DR. MINOT SAVAGE

PURE SPIRIT

When the pure Spirit shines who sees it?
Few, yea, only a very few!
For not many have the seeing eye.
Many see the light of the sun, the moon,
    the far-distant stars
And the light of the road-side lamp;
But only the pure in heart with the eye
    of love
Can see the light that shineth from
    pure Spirit.

I

VALUE OF COMPARATIVE STUDY

OUR object in surveying the world of religion and making a comparative study of it is not in any way to prove the supremacy of one religion over another, but to find a sympathetic chord which may serve as a common synthesis for all. When the great Parliament of Religions was convened in 1893 in connection with the Columbian Exposition held at Chicago, it met with no small opposition from the eminent dignitaries of the orthodox churches, and even from prominent laymen. Some thought it was a sacrilege to admit that there was any true religion other than Christianity. After much discussion and opposition, when this great

ideal of bringing diversified religions together became an actual fact, even then
many devout Christians candidly believed
that it was going to prove once for all the
supremacy of Christianity over all other
existing faiths, but its effect was quite the
contrary. It proved that noble ideas and
ideals were not exclusive to any country
or nation, but were present among all peoples of the earth.

Since the latter part of the nineteenth
century the comparative study of religion
has been somewhat in vogue. Independent
thinkers and learned men and women of
all nations are now strongly advocating
it; but, alas, in the major portion of litera-
ture which deals with comparative study,
we find a decidedly biased attitude. Some-
one starts with the idea of proving the exclusive superiority of his faith and having
this special aim in view, compares it with
other religious ideas and ideals. We can-

not expect any fairness in this method of dealing with the subject. Seeing through a biased mind is precisely like looking through colored glass. We cannot judge another, if our mind is already prejudiced; and it is no small problem to overcome our prejudices, no matter what our ethical theories are in regard to virtue and universal tolerance. With the rare exception of the few master-spirits of the world, it is difficult to find among mankind people who are free from prejudice and personal motives.

"Not every one that saith unto Me, 'Lord, Lord,' shall enter into the kingdom of Heaven, but he that doeth the will of my Father which is in Heaven." This saying of Jesus the Christ to my mind gives the key to the problem. It is not the dogmatic religion that ennobles us or widens our vision, but it is the practical religion, —"doing the will of the Father." Herein lies the whole secret. A man may proclaim charity in a loud tone, but if he lacks charity in his heart, what avails? A religion comes to us with a claim of universal love and brotherhood of mankind, but if it manifests aggression and bitterness towards those who do not follow its tenets, what lasting effect will it have upon our mind?

We may pretend and play the hypocrite in the world of commerce, in the field of science and politics, but in the realm of religion it is an utter impossibility. Some people claim supremacy because of the great antiquity their religion possesses; others for its being ultra-modern; but the vitality and truth of its thought are not proved by either of these means. The earnest soul invariably cries out for its practical value, and the practical value is found not in the crust of dogma, but in the living flame of life itself. What proves that we are living? It is life's motion that testifies to our existence, and if we possess high ideals, they must be equally evidenced through our life's activities. A person who possesses a great treasure and keeps it hidden, it neither profits him nor another. If you have a bright light, come out with it, let others see it and profit by it; but if you do not have it in your real and practical life, the theory of light is of little use either to yourself or to your fellow-beings.

This is my concept of practical religion. It makes a great ideal living and real, by looking upon which others find strength, inspiration, joy and peace. When we view the world of religion from this angle, at once it takes a universal aspect. Whether this ideal is realized through the study of the Jewish Kabala, the Sacred Book of the Babylonians, Egyptian Secret Codes, Greek Mythology, Chinese Wisdom, Vedic

Revelation, or through the Christian
Bible, is of small consequence. Men are
brothers only when they realize conscious-
ly that they have a common Father. Before this realization dawns in the individual heart, no amount of theories of
brotherhood will make one charitably in-
clined to another. "First seek ye the kingdom of Truth, all other things shall be
added unto you." "Know thyself that
thou mayst know all else." These are the
true and fundamental thoughts of the
spiritual world. It we do not abide by
them and follow their saving voice, we
are but led by the crooked paths of whims
and self-will; although we may claim our
alliance with the high and lofty religions
of the world. Our alliance must be from
within and primarily with the One Infinite Source, Who knows no division or
fraction, but is ever the same to all His
creatures.

II

CHRIST OF THE EAST

A S we stand on the watch-tower of life and observe the up-grade and down-grade of human destiny, we are at once struck forcibly what an impelling power religion holds over human life and what influence it exerts on civilization. On one hand nothing is more potent than religion to unite human lives; on the other hand nothing has greater power to divide the human family into separate groups. What is the cause of this dual aspect of religion? Religion itself, in its wide sense, is not dual. Its aim and objective are always the same, but our acceptance and application of what we call our particular religion creates endless diversity. It is due to this multiplicity of non-essentials that we are separated into so many distinct groups. It will not be necessary for me to seek far to illustrate this, for here in Christendom there are ample examples to be found through its varied expression in Christian denominations. Do they all follow the path of Christ? They all claim to do so. Yet keen observation and scrutiny will show us that they have little connection with one another except in name.

Ritual and dogma do not make religion, though religion sometimes finds these useful in its practical application But what grip dogma has upon most religious creeds! Perhaps it is due to this fact that we find more division than unity even in the same religion. When one wants to learn of Christ, one's natural inclination is to go to the institution which bears His name. Yet how difficult it is. Some represent Christ as a militant aggressor, some as a social reformer, some as an intolerant leader, according to their special prejudice. There arises even a greater difficulty when we try to find a point of contact between the personality of Jesus of Nazareth and those who claim to represent Him. So if we are earnestly seeking to solve this problem, we have no small difficulties to overcome.

Let me draw before you a picture of the Christ as He is conceived in the soul of the East. The mind of the Easterns conceives Him as a messenger of light. They clothe Him with robe of gentleness, with bearing majestic by divine right; they picture Him as the incarnate Spirit of love and divine loveliness,—lowly of heart, mighty of spirit, Brother, Friend and Saviour of man! You may say these very attributes are also applied by the Christians. What is the difference? There is

one very great and vital difference. Orthodox Christianity exalts Christ to the ex-
clusion of all other divine manifestations,
while the Eastern soul receives Him as the
cosmic Light, blending its harmony with
both past and present. Whichever concept we hold will have a marked influence
upon our life and destiny. For the one
invariably works for the destruction of
what is not its own, and the other for the
preservation and assimilation of what may
not seem at first sight to be its own. The
one holds to the dogmatic Christ, the
creed-bound Christ of organization and
institution; the other looks to that Christ
who is the soul of Divinity, who cannot be
partitioned off any more than we can par-
tition off the infinite sky. If the East
feels any rebellion, it is against dogmatic
Christianity.

If you were to ask me, are you a Christian? I should say no. If you were to ask

me, are you a Buddhist? I should again say no; yet I can say sincerely from my heart that I am a devout follower of both these ideals, and to me there is no difference between them. All great faiths are the expression of the one great cosmic Spirit coming down to man to show him his relationship with the Divine. The difficulty comes when we fail to bring these ideals into our life, then we can see nothing but differences. We even destroy each other in the name of God. Is this religion? Is it the theme of any religion that man should strike man, should destroy man, should create enemies and disturb the balance of the universe?

There was a time when people believed that if the whole world were converted to one religion, it would be saved. There are still those who believe that the salvation of the world depends on its being converted to Christianity. But the last war has

proved it to be otherwise. Was it fought
by the Christians in their religious zeal
against the non-Christians? No, it was
for the most part, Christian brothers cut-
ting each other's throats; Christian minds
scheming by diabolical means to annihi-
late one another. And what does it mean?
That it is not the sectarian acceptance of
any faith, no matter how lofty, which is
going to bring saving grace to the world.
It would be wonderful if all people could
be converted to the lofty and beautiful
teachings of Jesus of Nazareth, the Christ
of the Orient, the lowly, prayerful, devoted, yearning Christ who seeks divine
grace above all other things, who shows
man that his first and foremost duty is
to find God, to live for God, and to make
God a living presence in his life.

This is not to give you the picture of
another Christ. It is not to prove to you
that Christ went to India for a period of

time and studied there. Not at all! These things are of very little importance. Wisdom is never confined to any corner of the world, although it is true that the Orient has become symbolic of religion. Great Saviours and Seers have risen from the East. It is natural that they should, because the Eastern heart yearns primarily for spirituality.

In India if a man comes with a message hundreds of people will listen to him eagerly. If however he teaches love and exhibits hatred in his actions, if he preaches brotherhood and condemns with bitterness those who do not agree with him, at once they will say: "If your religion is true why do you not practise it? Prove your faith by your life and we will die for it." It is here the Eastern heart beats. It is here that we find the great difference between life and creed. A man who has touched the heart of God has touched the universal heart. He is no longer capable of being petty, small and fanatical, of being jealous or hateful. In India there is a tradition that if base metal is brought in contact with the philosopher's stone, it is transformed into gold and is no longer base. Even a sword brought in contact with that stone is at once transformed so that it can no more harm any one. The same is true of us.

Suppose we believe that we have a higher ideal than another? Are we going to conquer him by inferior means, by fighting him? Can we force him to change his ideal? The only way we can influence him is by our superior quality. In this way true religion becomes the most dominant factor in evolution. It does not go with gun and sword to destroy. By destructive means we never can do any good. If we have something beautiful or true, let us prove it by our life. What does Christ teach? He teaches love—love which over-comes hatred; not the love that sometimes loves and again hates, but the love which overrules all afflictions, all dualities and becomes the ideal. Is this ideal merely for those who profess Christianity? No, it is a world-ideal. God's spirit is cosmic, universal. It is the common heritage of humanity. One becomes a good Christian not by clinging to a special creed, but by living. Living the life is the basis of all religions. And this very theme is vividly illustrated by Lessing in his play called "Nathan the Wise," "Why, Nathan, you are a Christian," one of the characters exclaims in reply to certain noble thoughts expressed by the Jew. "What makes of me a Christian in your eyes makes you a Jew in mine," was Nathan's answer.

Can man ever say that his God is in-finite and then limit Him? Can it please his Deity for him to turn away from any

one, to shun any one, to condemn any one?
Will there be room in his heart after that
for divine love? Will his prayers be acceptable to God? How often Christ told
His disciples to go and make peace with
their brethren before placing their gifts
on the altar. Though we may have the
biggest church conceivable, though our
altar may be glittering with gold and dia-
monds, our offering will not be acceptable
to God if we have in our hearts aught
against any one.

There was a little cartoon which ap-
peared some years ago in Florence, Italy.
The import of it was that Christ came into
the world to-day and naturally went to
His own churches, churches which bore
His name, which claimed to be founded
upon His teaching. He entered them, but
the people were so engaged with ostenta-
tion that they had no time for the lowly
Christ; he was unable to draw their at-

tention, because they were too busy with
what they called Christianity and its prop-
agation. Then He went into the streets,
but the people were too occupied with their
own affairs to have time for Christ. Even
the poor people were so absorbed in their
poverty that they were not looking for
religion. So the lowly Christ went walking
and weeping through the wilderness.

Can we say Christianity is a failure?
A clergyman once remarked that it had
not yet been tried. It is not that we should
find fault with any religion. We can never
realize the ideals of any faith in its ex-
ternals. The heart of every religion. is
vibrant with life, but we have to reach that
heart; then we find it is always the self-
same Truth flowing through different
channels. India has never rejected a divine Incarnation and the reason is this:
in the Bhagavad-Gita, one of her most
holy and ancient Scriptures, the Lord de-

clares: "Whenever and wherever virtue
declines and vice prevails, then I embody
Myself. For the protection of the good
and for the destruction of the evil and for
the re-establishment of religion, I am born
from age to age." The Lord's promise is
not confined to India, or to any particular
place or time. All are His children.
This God of Vedic conception is universal
and infinite. He has only one heart and
in that heart there is love for all.

This Vedic ideal of God saturates the
whole of India's practical life. As soon
as we begin to live our Ideal, a strange
transformation takes place: our heart
grows quieter and more understanding.
We become incapable of doing anything
ignoble. The example of the bee is given
in India. The bee makes a great noise
until it has found the heart of the flower.
Once it has tasted the honey, it is quiet.
The same way is it with all the intolerance

and sectarian wars that are going on in the world,—it is because man has not touched the heart of religion. We never find the great spiritual teachers coming with aggressive spirit to convert the world. They live gently; their appeal is lowly and tender. But how often zealous followers distort their message of love and gentleness. We always make a mockery of our Ideal unless we live it.

Non-resistance of evil, one of the vital themes of Christ's teaching, can only be proved by our life. It is beautifully exemplified in the story of the Indian religious mendicant who was set upon and beaten by an ignorant man. He fell to the ground unconscious and lay there till his brothers from the monastery came and picked him up. They took him home and nursed him and, as he was returning to consciousness, one of them asked: "My brother, who is caring for you?" and he replied: "Verily, the same one who beat me." It was the feeling of oneness, the refusal to recognize any but the One, which animated him. Indian conception does not admit two forces,—one, God and the other, devil. There is only one infinite, all-abiding Spirit Who dwells within the hearts of all. When we worship Him, love Him, and draw close to Him, then do we find the fulfillment of life and a great realization of His oneness dawns within us. When the sun shines, the darkness vanishes; when the light of Spirit dawns within us, the bondage of materiality breaks.

The life of the world can be enriched by the life of the individual. We either bring a discordant note or we bring a note of harmony into this great universe by our life. We do not have to become preachers to spread the great Gospel of Truth; but we have to live, and as we live we create an atmosphere. A person feels exalted or he feels depressed on coming near us. Unconsciously we can hurt others and also unconsciously we can do them good. That is the Christ example. Let a man live, let his light shine, so that his Father in Heaven may be glorified through him. We should not act with any other motive. We should not pray to God merely because we are in despair. That is not the highest flight of religion. When we really feel hungry for it, thirsty for it, when we feel suffocated by materiality, then we naturally want to breathe in the open. That is the aspiration of the soul. We become spiritual because we are hungry for spiritual things. As a man thinks, so is he. If we hunger for the spiritual, it makes no difference where we live, we shall find the radiance,—the light that shines from Christ and from Buddha and from all the other Saviours.

It is only through superior living that

we make converts. Not by argument or
logic or any other material power do we
conquer human hearts, but always through
gentleness. Our love, our spirituality
radiate. That is my conception of Christ.
He brings inspiration because He comes
from God. He lives in God. He makes
no compromise. He lives the life. That
is His appeal. It not only brings benediction upon a few but upon all, because what
is good for the individual is good for the
whole, and we cannot progress unless we
are equally concerned in the welfare of
all our fellow-beings. There can be no
selfish happiness. That is the supreme
example in the lives of all great teachers.
Christ brings the message of love and it
must be realized through love. If we are
able to love so much that we recognize no
hatred at all in our hearts, then we shall
indeed feel the Christ heart within us, we
shall truly become a glowing example of

that Ideal. Even without word of mouth
we shall be able to fulfill our mission.
What have we to give to the world with
words unless our thoughts are the product
of spiritual realization? As we are dragged
into the whirl of outer life and scatter
our forces, we become more and more im-
poverished spiritually. That is the great
lack of to-day. We have all the things
that are outer, but we need the inner.

We should not change our faith. We do
not need to change it, because each faith
is part of the one great faith. Every church,
every creed, every religion, has at its heart
the glowing light of spiritual reality. The
Indian banyan tree is a very wonderful
example of the spiritual life. It keeps on
spreading and spreading till it becomes a
mighty forest. The same way it is in the
cosmic universe. There is only one God,
one religion, but it has many aspects.
Should we destroy any one of these be-

cause we are incapable of understanding it? In realizing the heart of religion, the spirit of it, we give a deathblow to all fanaticism and pettiness.

We should never lose faith either in Divinity or in humanity. Faith is a precious light and we should never be without it. It helps us to walk safely through the darkest hour of life. When we place our faith in Him Who is the Source of All; when our mind and heart are filled with the consciousness that we are children of the One, should we not be capable of doing greater good to our own kinsmen? For when we realize our divine heritage, our common Parent, we are invariably related to each other as we are related to Him, and this becomes the practical basis for true and ideal brotherhood.

III

CHRIST AND ORIENTAL IDEALS

HOW often it is supposed that Christian ideals and Oriental ideals are alien to each other and can never converge; that the adoption of one means the abandonment of the other, like roads going in opposite directions. But this idea can only exist so long as we remain on the outskirts of the religious domain, in the realm of creed and form. When we judge East and West from external appearances only, then we find great differences; but they are chiefly in manners and customs and not in the fundamental principles which lie beneath. There is vast difference between the outer expression of religion

and the actual assimilation of its essence;
and most of our misunderstandings and
dissensions arise from variance in forms.
Even to-day there can be found men and
women in India who illustrate the Christ-
Ideal wonderfully in their lives, although
they may never have heard about Jesus
of Nazareth or read the Bible, and might
refuse to accept the Christian creed. What
is a creed? The Supreme Ideal can never
be labelled or represented by any one
creed. Living the life is its only true interpretation; and the East is peculiarly
adapted for this. As an eminent Christian Divine, Rev. Cuthbert Hall, has
forcibly expressed it, in speaking to the
Hindus themselves:

"The contemplative life is the life that
puts thought above action, the invisible
above the visible, as the major interest of
existence; that pays homage first to the
mind and the things of the mind; after-

ward to the body and the things of the
body. The life of action is not incompatible with the life of contemplation, but
subordinate to it. And especially is the
life of materialistic action subordinate;—
the struggle of competitive acquisition,
lust after riches, pride of display, arrogance of possession, scheming ingenuity
to override the interests or the efforts of
another, so as to accumulate wealth. From
this the contemplative life turns wearily
aside, asking only to be left at leisure to
think its way onward to the goal of God.
May I say that I seem to have found in
the East the natural home of the contemplative life? Its value, its appropriateness for man, its ennobling harmony with
man's nature and destiny, its abiding satisfactions as against feverish struggle for
things and short-lived enjoyment of them,
many of the West have known. And
many more in these latter days, jaded with

the quest of the visible, are seeking the
path of contemplation. But behind you
and your Seers lies the long Indian sum-
mer of the soul, thousands of years of the
contemplative life. It has given you certain elements of personality, and certain
qualifications for world efficiency which
misguided imitation of our Western ways
could only imperil. You have been Orientals since the dawn of the world. Continue to be Orientals forever, till the
world's last twilight closes in the final
darkness. Cling to the contemplative life:
your glorious heritage, your peculiar
strength. It has given you elements of
personality of which the West stands in
need and shall one day come seeking at
your hand. It has given you repose,
gentleness, patience, gravity, noble in-
difference alike to material possession and
material privation, eternal remembrance
of things that eye hath not seen nor ear

heard, which God hath prepared for them that love Him."

Religion in the East is not a matter of belief in doctrine, dogma, or creed; it is being and becoming; it is actual realization. Faithful practice alone can bring true knowledge of God. No theory or creed can be accepted until it has been verified by practice. What theory can succeed without solid knowledge behind it, that is, knowledge based on experience? And who can shake our faith when we have true knowledge? It was this which Christ meant when he gave the parable of the two houses: one built on the rock, the other on the sand, typifying the two lines of the religious life, the one of theory or mere belief, the other of practice. In the Hindu teaching we find a similar parable of two servants, who worked in the garden of a rich man. One of them was lazy and idled away his time, accomplish-

ing nothing; but when the master came
he met him with flattering devotion and
praised the beauty of his person; while
the other labored tirelessly and at the
coming of his master said little, but bringing the fruit and flowers he had raised,
he laid them humbly at his feet. Is it
difficult to say with which one the master
was more pleased?

In order to gain spiritual knowledge and
strength, we must work faithfully; and
we must use the same energy, diligence
and tenacity that we now expend for our
bodily existence. So long as spiritual cul-
ture remains secondary to us, we cannot
expect the highest achievement on any
plane; for this, the sages declare, is the
basic rock upon which all true knowledge
and growth must rest. That is the reason
why Christ taught as a fundamental lesson: "Seek ye first the kingdom of God
and His righteousness and all these things

shall be added unto you"; and why the ancient Aryans of India in their oldest Scriptures asked and sought to answer the question: "What is that, by knowing which all else may be known?" "What is the basis and ultimate goal of the universe?" These Rishis or Truth-Seers found out the necessity of first "proving all things" through experience, thus making knowledge a part of one's being. We may talk of Christ and go to church, but unless we apply His teaching in our lives, how far are we from the Christ-Ideal. We must become the thing itself; if we merely talk of it, we are no better than parrots. As Christ Himself declares: "Not every one that saith unto me, 'Lord, Lord' shall enter into the kingdom of heaven; but he that doeth the will of my Father which is in heaven." A religious teacher in India is never judged by his power of eloquence, but by the silent example of his life and character. His chief instruction is given not in words but in actions, and for that reason it is the more potent.

The East holds that to become spiritual we must make our thoughts, words and actions harmonious—that is, our whole being must work without friction or contradiction. This is only possible through right-thinking. Thoughts can pollute us as much as words or acts; therefore we must first spiritualize our thoughts; then alone will our words and acts be pure. Otherwise, what avail? The Hindu Scriptures declare, "What a man thinks, that he becomes"; so also we read in the Bible, "As a man thinketh in his heart so is he." For this reason, Vedanta forbids us to dwell on the thought of sin; because sin can never beget righteousness. No one can ever gain strength by brooding over his weakness. Hence, Vedanta tells us: "Call no man a sinner. All are children of Immortal Bliss. Let each one awaken his divine nature by constantly holding his thought on the Ideal." Christ makes the same appeal when He says: "Be ye therefore perfect, even as your Father which is in Heaven is perfect." Some believe that this is possible only for a Christ; but, according to Vedanta, the Saviours and prophets come especially to show by their example how all men can attain perfection. Man possesses within himself the germs of perfection, he has only to manifest it. He is already inherently perfect. Why then talk of sin? To think of ourselves as sinners cannot be the Christ-Ideal; otherwise, why should He have told us to be perfect like the Father in heaven?

This conception of the Fatherhood of God did not originate with Christ, as is generally supposed. As far back as the earliest Vedic Scriptures (at least 2000

B. C.) we find the Aryans of India address-
ing God as Father; and the idea was introduced into Palestine nearly half a century before Christ by Rabbi Hillel, who
it is known had imbibed it from the
Greeks.   Christ, however, made it one of
the fundamental principles of His teaching, and thus it has become a cardinal
doctrine of the Christian church.   Out of
this idea of the Fatherhood of God naturally springs the conception of the brotherhood of man.   But very often we forget
the first and vainly try to realize the second.   Yet how can we relate ourselves to
anyone as a brother, unless we know the
Father?   The true idea of philanthropy,
of charity, of love towards all cannot
come to us until we know God's relationship to us and to every living being.   Before we can fully believe that man is our
brother, we must know that God is our
Father.   That is why Christ gave as the

first commandment: "Love the Lord thy
God with all thy heart, with all thy mind
and with all thy soul"; and as the second:
"Love thy neighbor as thyself." The story
told of Socrates and the Hindu philosopher
teaches the same lesson. Socrates, it is
said, when asked by the Indian sage,
"What is the chief aim of life?" answered,
"The study of man." Whereupon the sage
replied, "How can you know man before
you have known God?"

So long as we deal with the fragments
of the universe, we see only differences and
cannot hope to attain harmony; but when
we come to know the essence, the stupen-
dous Whole of which all these various
fragments are parts, then we realize oneness and true brotherhood becomes possible. Christ taught, "Love thy neighbor
as thyself"; and the Hindu sages, going
one step further, tell us why we should
thus love our neighbor. They say, "Thou

art That"; that is, in essence you and your
neighbor are one and the same; therefore
to hurt your neighbor is to hurt yourself.
The recognition of this naturally leads to
the non-resistance of evil, upon which
Christ laid such stress. We can never
hope to practice true non-resistance until
we have found that from which all things
originate and are able to perceive the unity
underlying all the diversity of the phe-
nomenal world. "He is, indeed, wise who
can see One in the world of many," the
Vedas declare. As long, however, as we
live on the plane of duality, so long it is
impossible for us to attain this wisdom.

A man cannot help resisting evil as long
as he is conscious of it. He, who being
conscious of evil, does not resist it, is
either a hypocrite or weak-minded. But
the Christ-Ideal of non-resistance of evil,
like that of Vedanta, means that we tran-
scend it; that we no longer recognize evil

as an independent existence, but that we only recognize One God, Who is in every animate and inanimate object. This is wonderfully exemplified in the life of Jesus of Nazareth. All His work, all His miracles, all His sufferings and all His glory were based on this one supreme fact. He never forgot for one moment that His Father in Heaven was the only Doer, the sole basis of this universe; that all happenings good or bad, pleasant or painful, were wholly in accordance with His will.

Until we have this realization of oneness with the Supreme, it is not possible to rise above all differences and feel true love for our fellow-men. Without it, our efforts in philanthropy and reform can never succeed. We cannot bring humanity together by striving to destroy the outer differences. As far as the essence is concerned, there are no differences; and perfect harmony is attained only when we realize this great truth. Then alone we pick up the thread which binds us all together like pearls on a string, and it becomes possible for us to love even our enemies, as Christ, Buddha and all divine Incarnations have taught. "He who perceives all beings as the Self, for him how can there be delusion or grief, when he sees oneness everywhere?" (*Isa-Upanishad.*)

The idea of non-injury is common to all the great teachers of the world. "In half a verse I shall tell thee that which has been declared in numberless holy texts; that is, virtue consists in doing good to others and hurting others is the only vice." (*Vedic Scriptures.*) We must purify our heart by loving and harmonious thoughts before we can enter the kingdom of heaven. Christ tells us: "If thou bring thy gift to the altar and there rememberest that thy brother hath aught against thee; leave there thy gift before the altar and go thy way; first be reconciled to thy brother and then come and offer thy gift." This belief in the necessity of making peace before any act of worship is so strong in India, that they never begin any spiritual study or religious ceremony without pronouncing that *Santi-patha* or "peace-verse"; for they know that if there is not peace in the heart, it is not worthy to take the name of the Lord or offer anything to Him, nor can it hope to reap any blessing. We must root out all feeling of hatred before we can know Spirit. As Buddha declares: "Hatred does not cease by hatred at any time: hatred ceases by love. This is the old rule."

The great difference between Vedanta and Christianity is that Vedanta declares Truth to be one without a second; It is eternal and all-inclusive and cannot be limited by time, place or personality; the Christ-Ideal has always existed and will always exist, because it stands for a state and not for an individual. The Christians, on the other hand, claim that Christ is the only-begotten Son of God, that before Him God had never incarnated—that the whole Truth is centralized in this one manifestation, and those who do not accept Him are regarded as heathen with no hope of salvation. Vedanta says, how can that be? Can we ever limit the limitless Absolute? Can the Infinite be fully represented by any one finite form? It admits that Christ is one of the Incarnations, but not the only one; that before Him there were other divine manifestations, and that they will continue to come according to the need of humanity.

Such divine Incarnations occur whenever and wherever there is need for spiritual regeneration. There come times when materialistic thought overruns a nation and spirituality becomes a mockery, existing only in words and theories, in empty doctrines and forms; then we need a living example of virtue to reveal to us once more the eternally-existing Truth; and the Vedas call such God-men Revealers or Seers of Truth or *Avataras,* "Embodied Truth." It is not that they discover the Truth, but they reveal It; or in other words, they tear off the veil of worldliness which has for the time being hidden It. They do not give a new message; they only repeat the one already given, but forgotten. As Jesus Himself declared: "Think not that I am come to destroy the law or the prophets: I am not come to destroy, but to fulfill." The only differences we find in the messages of the different Saviours lie not in their fundamental principles, but in their outer expression, which is shaped according to the need of the age, country and people where the Incarnation takes place.

Sectarianism creates war and intolerance everywhere; but the Christ-Ideal, when lived, brings perfect harmony and universal tolerance, whether in the East or in the West. As the Rev. Cuthbert Hall again says: "As I grew to apprehend the qualities of the Oriental consciousness, I saw their potential value for the higher interpretation of the Christian religion. It became clear to me that in the Soul of the East are powers and gifts which stand in a significant relation to the higher truths of Christianity, correspondences which cannot be accidental, between the most sublime aspects of the religion of Christ and the most sublime qualities of the Eastern soul. Many times during the former visit among you I found myself exclaiming, how marvelously is the East qualified to be the interpreter of Christian mysteries; and how marvelously does the profound essence of Christian belief lend

itself to the modes of Oriental consciousness. Is there not here evidence of divine
intention, long unrealized? While the
West has heretofore regarded Christianity
as its own, an indigenous growth that
might with difficulty be introduced to the
East as an exotic, can it be that the Oriental consciousness is, in fact, the natural
soil of this divine plant, and that at last,
after many centuries, from the fruitful
ground of the Eastern soil, this seed of
God is to spring to the perfect type and
bear fruit a hundred-fold?"

We too often forget that Christ Himself was an Oriental. The Essenes, we
know, had a great influence on the life of
Jesus. John the Baptist himself was an
Essene; and it is now admitted by many
scholars that the foundation of the Order
of the Essenes was directly due to the influence of the Buddhist monks, who were
sent out as missionaries by the great In-

dian Emperor, Asoka, about 250 B. C. They came to Palestine, but following their habitual constructive method, they did not seek to proselytize. They merely lived a life of holiness and loving service to others without creating any antagonism; and they won followers through the force and beauty of their character, inspiring them to take up a similar life of simplicity and renuniciation, such as we see embodied in the rule of the Essenes and set forth in the life and teaching of Jesus.

This has been from the beginning the method of the Aryans of India. They have always believed that there was no reason to condemn any faith or ideal, no matter how crude it might appear. Universal tolerance is the dominant note of their teaching. "He is One without a second," manifesting in the form of a Christ, a Krishna, a Buddha, a Zoroaster; and those who follow sincerely any one of these manifestations will surely reach the final goal of Truth. "In whatever way men worship Me, in the same way I fulfill their desires. O Partha in every way men follow my Path," the Lord declares in the Bhagavad-Gita.

The attitude of Vedanta is that all is One Universal Spirit. The same Truth exists in every faith and when we follow one truly, we follow all; because the same note of truth is at the heart of all; and when we touch it in one, all the others vibrate in sympathy and perfect harmony is the result. As long as we find fault with any faith or denounce any man as a heathen, we are far from being religious. A child of God is never a heathen. Unless we love all of God's children, how can we please the Father? "He maketh His sun to rise on the evil and on the good, and sendeth rain on the just and on the unjust."

When we comprehend the true divine beauty of any one of the great ideals, our prejudices and religious antagonisms disappear. The practical application of the teaching of any one always takes us nearer to the essence of all and destroys the delusion out of which sectarianism grows. Unless we live the life in accordance with our special Ideal, we remain at a great distance from our Master and are not worthy to call ourselves His followers. How can you know what Christ stood for unless you live a Christ-life? If you do not represent His teaching in your thoughts and actions, you merely drag down the Ideal. To take His name without following His teaching does not make a man a Christian. Vedanta declares that we must never compromise with the Ideal, we must never bring it down to our limited plane; we must raise ourselves to it. We must devote our whole life to realizing it;

and if we fail, we must blame ourselves, not the Ideal, recognizing our own limitations.

God is infinite but He assumes different forms for the sake of His devotees; yet the Infinite, according to Vedanta, can never be fully expressed in name and form. Therefore the sages define Him as both personal and impersonal. He is beyond mind and speech. "He is One without a second, but sages comprehend Him differently and call Him by different names." He is all that we are capable of grasping, as well as all that is beyond our comprehension; for how can the Infinite be fully grasped by the finite mind? Even the divine Incarnations can be only partial manifestations of the Infinite-Absolute; and because no one personality or creed can satisfy all mankind, every phase of religion, from the crudest form of symbolism to the highest conception of Absolute

Truth, is given a place in Vedanta. Max Muller admits this when he says: "Thus the Vedanta philosophy leaves to every man a wide sphere of real usefulness, it has room for every religion, nay, it embraces them all."

Let us look upon life from the God point of view. Then all these outer differences will vanish and perfect peace and harmony will reign. True religious growth consists in expansion, not in contraction; it is inclusive and not exclusive. Let us cease to try to override those who differ from us in belief. Let us work on the constructive basis of love and tolerance, and thus prove ourselves worthy of our Ideal, whatever may be His name.

IV

THE SPIRIT OF CHRIST

THE Spirit of Christ cannot be realized merely by belonging to a church.
It comes from something in the heart,
and only to those who "do the Will of
the Father," as Christ Himself said. The
divine Will is one and universal, and when
we unite ourselves with that Will, we work
for the universal good. The Christ-Ideal
is not confined to Christendom, as the sky
overhead does not cover one land or one
people only. Thus there lived in India
not many years ago a Brahmin saint, who
had no contact with Christianity and yet
who so far exemplified the teaching of
Jesus: "Him that taketh away thy cloak
forbid him not to take thy coat also," that

the following incident among many others
is told of him:

One day a thief entered his little hut
and gathered into a bundle the few cook-
ing pots and provisions which he had
there; but hearing the saint approach, the
man dropped the bundle and ran. The
saint, picking up the bundle, ran after
him. The thief, believing that he was being pursued, ran faster and faster, but
finally the saint overtook him and laid the
bundle before him, saying: "Take it, it
is yours." The exhausted thief looked at
the saint wonderstruck. Then lifting the
bundle, he followed the saint back to his
hut and became one of his most ardent disciples. From such examples we must realize that religion is not merely subscribing
to a creed; it is wholly a matter of living
and feeling.

That one who is capable of feeling the
joys and griefs of all other men as his

own, he alone is a true example of the
Christ-Spirit whatever may be the form
of his faith. When a follower of Christ
shuts his heart against a child of God in
any faith, he makes a mockery of his religion, because it is contrary to what
Christ taught. Christ was willing to sacrifice His life even, in the service of God.
When God so dominates our heart that
we are willing also to give up our life,
then we are true to the Ideal which He
preached. We must create within us an
atmosphere of holiness and loving brotherhood which will unite us, first with God
and then with our fellowmen.

At the present time we are very proud
of our mechanical inventions and social
progress; but we do not see that our spiritual ideals have become faded. We look
upon religion as a matter of tradition and
as an important factor in maintaining social order. But religion is something more

than that. When we are put through the greatest difficulties and do not grow faint-hearted, that is religion. And whether we are Christian, Mohammedan, Hindu or Jew, if we can maintain the same living faith in God, the same ungrudging love for His children in all circumstances, then we are religious.

How do we know there is a God until we have proved it? Until our soul has communed with Him and lived close to Him, we cannot be absolutely sure that He exists. Religion is a question of plunging within and living with the Ideal. When the Christ-Spirit shall truly seize the human heart, then will dawn a new era of civilization. Whenever the world is thwarted and saddened, it looks for a new vision; but when all goes well, it settles back into the old way. It is natural to turn to God when we are forsaken by men and misunderstood by friends; but we do

not truly worship Him until we come
seeking nothing of Him. We must out-
grow the habit of bargaining, of asking a
fair return in personal benefit for our service to God. That attitude always limits
our capacity to express the Divine. It
also limits the power of God to bless us;
for He cannot give us more than we are
willing to take; and if we pray for some
special thing, setting our heart on that,
He cannot bestow on us a greater blessing. That is why Christ's prayer was:
"Not my will, but Thine be done."

The divine Incarnations are spiritual
sight-givers. They are true redeemers,
but they represent a state of being, not
separate personalities. The differences we
find in these Messengers are very small.
There are differences in language and in
the detail of the methods used, which are
accounted for by differences in the speech
and customs of the people among whom

they came; but fundamentally they all proclaim the same spirit of love and tolerance. Krishna (1400 B. C.), Buddha and Laotze (500 B. C.), Christ and all the other Saviours give the same message. The differences which appear spring from the varying human interpretations applied to them; because the followers of the Great Ones have not been able to realize the ideals which their special Masters set forth.

There is no need of intolerance. There is one infinite Godhead and infinity is all-inclusive. If people would bear this in mind, we would at once eliminate all these ideas of difference between East and West, North and South; and we would see all living beings as parts of one human family. Whether a saint has become saintly by following the teachings of Christ or Buddha or Krishna makes no difference. What do we gain by hatred or condemnation? We harm ourselves more than any one. If we can realize these deeper facts, we shall shake off a great deal which is non-essential in our lives.

Christ taught that before we lay our gift on the altar, we must go and make peace with our brother; that is, we must remove all that is harsh and impure from our heart. The Vedic sages gave the same teaching. We all think how wonderful it would be to have the brotherhood of man; but this will never be possible until we have realized the Fatherhood of God; and we cannot realize the Fatherhood of God until we see all men as children of one Father. All ideas of difference in caste, creed, race or nation must go down. We are children of the one God. It is an absolute fact. The moment we truly feel ourselves to be His children, there will come to us a new power for good.

Those who are not faint-hearted, who

are not content merely with intellectual gifts, but who have great hearts free from all pettiness, must work for this larger ideal of unity. And when this broader vision comes to us, do not let us talk merely, but let us go onward and forward until we realize it in our life. An Ideal is something to be carried with us and put into practice at every moment. It requires unshakable faith, however, to abide by any Ideal. Christ's faith in His Father did not waver even on the cross. When this comes, we can walk through fire and overcome insurmountable obstacles.

The Christ Spirit cannot exist where there is the least self-seeking. We learn this lesson from the life of every Saviour. The great Saviours gave their message, whether men received it or not, and they were ready to sacrifice their life for the very ones who denounced them. So must we do. When like Christ we can disregard

the petty things of life and go bravely on
—that is what will give us real strength.

The more we can live up to the Ideal
which was in Christ, the more shall we
become one with the Universal Ideal. We
must not think that our duty ends when
we have heard the teachings of a great
Saviour. Our duty is not ended until we
have fashioned our lives after the life of
the Ideal; and made all our thoughts,
words and deeds like unto His Whom we
worship. These Great Ones came as men
to show that what they have done we can
do. Outwardly they may appear like human beings, but inwardly their heart and
mind are all full of God. So must our
heart be full of God also, if we would manifest the Christ-Spirit.

Let us try to reflect in our life all the
beautiful lessons set forth in the life of
Jesus. Forgiveness, love, fortitude—these
are the lessons we learn from Him; and

as we become imbued with them, His Spirit will abide more and more with us and grow, until we shall truly realize the power of His words: "Be ye perfect as your Father in heaven is perfect." When everything is still, when the world in us lies asleep, then is the Christ-Spirit born in us. It is in the moments of serenity and silence that we feel its presence. Let us strive to awaken that Spirit in our hearts. Let us connect ourselves wholly with God. As we live in Spirit, we shall be born anew in Spirit.

The Christ-Spirit does not come to us only on certain occasions. When we seek Him, He becomes our constant companion. We are very much alone so long as we depend on worldly association. Human friendship changes because it is based on changing things, but divine friendship never changes. If we lean upon that, we shall never feel forsaken. We are not strong in any other way, but only when we put our whole trust in the Divine.

No matter where we stand or what we are, if we can kindle the fire of devotion in us, that will burn all our impurities to ashes. We must, however, sacrifice our foolish egotism and vanity. We must be able to say, as Christ said, "Thy Will be done." Also we must never grow faint-hearted or lose faith either in God or in our own higher nature. Let us pray from the depth of our being that we may grow daily in purity and holiness and that we may be worthy of our Ideal. Without His strength we are weak. Without His support, we stumble. But if we call upon Him with our whole heart, He will surely come and manifest His Spirit in us. Then shall we realize that we are born of Spirit and that our true life is eternal and infinite.

V

UNIVERSAL TOLERANCE

THE Christ-Ideal to me has a universal appeal. In the East there are people who have neither read the Bible nor come in contact with Christians, yet their lives exemplify to a remarkable degree what was taught by Jesus of Nazareth. This must make us realize that like the sky over every head the real spirit of religion is universal; but through our narrow vision we limit it and make a mockery of it. It does not matter what we profess. Name and form have very little to do with the soul of religion. It is all-embracing and we feel it in our heart. According to my conception, the import of the teachings of Christ and of

all the great Lights of the spiritual world
is one and only one. Their sole aim is to
show us how we may bring the living
presence of our Ideal into our consciousness and actions. Whoever does this is a
follower of the Christ-Ideal, whatever may
be the nature of his creed. It is living according to our highest concept which
makes us worshippers of God. If we do
not do this, praising our special form of
faith and exalting it above all others will
not avail much. It is only our life which
will uphold it. If we do not glorify it in
our life and activity, we may talk of universal love and tolerance and of all the
beautiful things taught in the great Bibles
of the world and by the great Teachers,
but our words will not carry weight. It is
our life alone which counts, and a divine
Incarnation comes to show us how through
concentrated thought and action we may
unite ourselves with Divinity.

He comes to point the way Godward;
to help us break down all the fictitious bar-
riers of caste and creed which divide us.
When we come in contact with such manifestations, we see how quickly the non-
essentials vanish and the ice of misunder-
standing melts away. It is the sun of
wisdom which melts all coldness from the
human heart and unites us. And that is
the only real worship. It is not in theory,
it is not in dogma that religion consists;
it is in feeling and realizing. That is the
dominant note running through all Vedic
philosophy.

It brings a greater blessing when we
take a divine ideal from the broader point
of view than when we confine it to any
one form. In India there are many who
are regarded as divine Incarnations. The
Vedic Scriptures declare that whenever
virtue subsides and vice prevails, when
people become immersed in materialism

and selfishness, then the Lord embodies Himself and once more manifests the Truth. He comes whenever and where-ever there is need. There is no limit set for His coming; and however and when-ever He comes, it is always the same In-finite Being. There can be no essential difference between the spirit of Christ and the spirit of Buddha or the spirit of any manifestation before or since. There is only one Absolute Being and all divine Manifestations are from that Source. In a family a father may appear one day in one garment and on another day in anoth-er, and the children would be foolish in-deed if they did not recognize him in the different garments he might wear. We are equally foolish when we fail to recognize the one universal Father under all His various forms, and condemn those who invoke Him by other names.

An interesting story is told in India of

a fanatic who worshipped Siva, the third
person of the Hindu Trinity. He was so
ardent a follower of his Deity that he did
not want to hear any other name of God.
He wished to exclude every aspect of Divinity except his own. At last the Lord
Himself said: "I must teach this man that
it is I Who manifest Myself in all forms,
that there is no difference between one and
another." So He came to him in a form
which was half Siva and half Vishnu. The
devotee was half pleased and half dis-
pleased. He shut one eye and with the
other looked at the Siva side only. Even
this visible proof did not convince him.
The children in the street, seeing that he
was a fanatic and that it irritated him to
hear any other name than that of Siva,
began shouting other sacred names whenever he passed. This made him so des-
perate that he hung bells on his ears to
drown the sound of their voices.

Many among us are sincere and fervent in upholding our Ideal, but in our zeal we overlook the fact that the whole universe is part of that Ideal and that all men, of whatever nation or faith, are just as much children of God as we are. If we are not kind, tender, loving and forgiving towards all, we have no share in the religion we profess. Jesus the Christ taught this through His life, through His self-abnegation and His all-embracing love, a love which was not confined merely to those who followed Him and loved Him and were related to Him. Gautama Buddha, who was called the Compassionate One, preached: "You must so adjust your heart that you long for the welfare of all beings, including the happiness of your enemies." Universal love and universal tolerance—these are the notes which sound through the teachings of all great Incarnations. They uphold these transcendent ideals not only in their words, but in their actions. They make them real by living them. We struggle and stumble and fail; then we imagine that these lofty ideals are not attainable for us. Through such divine manifestations, however, we see that they are attainable, that it is possible for a man to rise to so great a height of spiritual reality that, when he is struck by an enemy, he not only controls himself and does not strike back, but he actually loves that enemy.

We do not prove our greatness by belonging to this religion or to that religion. We prove it by our faithfulness, by our loyalty to our Ideal, and by carrying our Ideal into our life. The man who forgives most, who loves most, is a true Christian. He has reached the Christ-Ideal, and also he has reached the universal spirit. He perceives that there is no difference between one child of God and another. There are many paths which lead to the same goal, and only by realizing this do we realize true brotherhood.   Not through exclusiveness, not through denunciation, not through fanatical zeal of any kind, can the spirit of brotherhood be attained.   It is right for us to be devoted to our Ideal; but do not let us attach too much importance to outer form and creed.   Let us lay all stress on the inner life, for it is the inner life alone which counts.   We must try to unfold that life.   So long as we lack it, we may hold all the lofty ideals given in the Sacred Books, but what good will it do?

We cannot accept anything truly until we know it, and we know the truths given in the Scriptures and by the Great Ones through our inner life.   That alone enables us to read the book of Truth unerringly. It is the spirit of religion which we need to touch.   We shall always find difference in forms. So long as men cling to these forms, one will say: "My creed is the only creed through which you can attain salvation." And another will make the same claim for his creed. Which one shall we believe? They speak with equal fervor and devotion. In this world of diversity necessarily there is a great variety of temperaments. One person likes to worship God by elaborate ceremonials, another feels irritated by ritual. He prefers philosophy and reason. Should he not have a share in God's life also? God has provided for all amply. His storehouse is inexhaustible, and one who has touched that Divine Being knows that he cannot exhaust It or confine It within one special creed.

An ordinary man says, "This is my religion, that is your religion; this is my land, that is your land." The spirit of wisdom, however, teaches us that this "mine" and this "thine" do not exist in the realm of reality. When we merge our life in the universal life and unite our hearts with the inexhaustible Source, we rise above the sense of separateness. That is why we must seek the kingdom of heaven first. When we have found it, selfishness drops away from us; all harshness, all discordant feelings disappear; and we live altogether in another sphere. That kingdom is already within us, but we must discover it. We cannot discover it, however, through any book or creed. No one can reveal it to us. An earnest, yearning spirit alone will give us access to it. We must voluntarily, ardently, hungrily seek it; then we shall find it. There is no other way.

There is no one who can eat for us and give us the benefit of the nourishment; how, then, can any one do our thinking about God and give us the vision? It is not possible. All the great Seers tell us to know the Truth and the Truth will make us free. This knowing is accomplished only by going within our own being. It is there we realize that our true heritage is God and that we are children of Divinity. Whenever we try to keep any one out, we strike a discordant note. It takes us away from our Ideal, even though apparently we have devotion for It. Real religion teaches us the fundamental principles of life—love and tolerance for all humanity. When we bind our hearts to these principles, then Divinity shines through us and for us from within and from without; all quarters are pervaded and permeated by that Divine influence and we find that we have risen above the God of tradition.

When that inner Truth begins to shine, then we feel what is true brotherhood. How can we realize the brotherhood of man until we have learned something of the Fatherhood of God? Do we really feel that God is our Infinite Father? If He is, then all are His children and we have no right to raise our voice against the least of His creatures. When we gain this universal feeling, we have reached the threshold of true religion. Before that we merely talk theories. The way to gain it is from within, not by making outside adjustments and changes.

There are many to-day who claim that religion is not proving successful. There are ministers even who believe that we must have more attractions and amusements in the churches to draw the public. People are not drawn in that way to the altar of God. Such things may attract them for the moment, but Truth alone can draw the heart. Truth can reach us, however, only when we have thrown away the blemish of selfishness and all the things which now hide the Truth. That gem of Truth must shine clearly; and when it shines in our life, when we see all things in Truth, then our small, harsh, unworthy feelings will be destroyed and our hearts will be filled with love and universal tolerance.

VI

THE PRACTICE OF THE
CHRIST-IDEAL

GOD manifests in the form of a man that man may comprehend what God is. The Absolute is declared to be unknowable and unthinkable, hence He is beyond the reach of the human mind. But to make it possible for man to understand Him, He assumes personal aspects and comes as a Christ or a Buddha. This is what is meant by a divine Incarnation. Such a manifestation serves as the connecting link between God and man. He is divine enough to be in touch with God and human enough to be in touch with man, so that man may realize divine things through Him.

To grasp truly what an Incarnation is, however, we must have like qualities and show them forth in our lives. The words and actions of a great teacher no one can wholly understand until he has risen to the same plane of spiritual consciousness. When we have the same thing in us that was in Christ or in Buddha, then it is possible for us to comprehend what they taught. Until then, what they say and do must remain a closed chapter. We can never draw the picture of a great Being either to satisfy ourselves or others until we have the same qualities. One who speaks of Christ must himself be Christ-like in his life, love and wisdom, else his words will carry but little weight.

When our inner being becomes attuned with the Supreme then alone can we express Him in our words and actions. That is why all the divine Seers unanimously declare the absolute need of the practical application of spiritual teaching. "Being and becoming" is the watchword of the sages. Let your light shine, that light within, the light of your living soul, let that shine forth, then all the clouds of doubt and ignorance will be dispelled and you will be able to comprehend the Divine. When your heart becomes pure you must see God. No one can prevent you. No church, no priest, nothing can keep you from seeing Him.

To the majority the Christ-consciousness or the direct perception of Truth seems something unattainable. But that cannot be. What has happened once will happen again. What has been done can be done: that is the law. The purpose of a divine Incarnation is not merely to manifest His superhuman and miraculous powers, but to point out to mankind by His life and example the goal of existence and man's divine birthright. Saviours do not come to proclaim things which are impossible for man to attain. No, we think them impossible because we do not try to practice them, so our religion degenerates into a blind and thoughtless acceptance of certain fixed forms and doctrines. When religion thus becomes a matter of mere belief and exists only as a theory, having lost its living quality, then God incarnates in human form to re-establish spirituality and destroy materialism.

Thus God manifests Himself at different periods of history in order to give tangible knowledge of His divine nature. To make things that are incomprehensible to the finite mind, comprehensible, He takes finite form. He comes not to display His own glory; no, but to show man how as man he can manifest God; or as St. Augustine puts it—"God was made man that man might become God."

The purpose of the life and teaching of

a great Saviour is to open man's eyes to his own higher Self, to awaken more love for God than for mundane things; or in other words, to make a mortal feel conscious of his immortal nature. In order to gain this consciousness and make it a part of our being we must learn to practice the Christ-Ideal in our everyday life. We must picture it. We must make it living to our heart. We must feel its reality. As we cultivate this habit of feeling the living Presence within, our vision will become more and more open to subtle spiritual facts, which otherwise remain vague and unreal.

People's sight varies. Things which we may see plainly are not visible to the blind man; so in the days of our inner blindness, we cannot see God or understand His manifestations. This was the case with the Scribes and Pharisees. Although they were scholarly men, possessing the full knowledge of the letter, yet they failed to understand Christ because they lacked that inner light which comes only through practice of the spirit. With most people the spiritual life is a matter of theory. They have just a little intellectual grasp of it; that is quite enough for them. But practice is the whole of it; and not having practical experience in religion, we can never penetrate the inner depths of anything.

One man may go to church, pray and sing hymns in the name of Jesus, appearing righteous, but this cannot make him spiritual or bring him blessing so long as he does not manifest the teaching in his life; and there may be another who may never go to a church or utter the name of Christ, but who through the practice of holiness and purity so embodies and radiates the Christ-spirit that he becomes a living symbol of the Christ-life. Such a soul alone truly honors Him and proves a worthy follower. As it is said in one of the Buddhist Sacred Books: "Now it is not thus, Ananda, that the Tathagata (Incarnate One) is rightly honored, reverenced, venerated, held sacred and revered. But the brother or the sister, the devout man or the devout woman, who continually fulfills all the greater and the lesser duties, who is correct in life, walking according to the precepts, it is he who rightly honors, reverences, venerates, holds sacred and reveres the Incarnate One with the worthiest homage."

We do not honor our Saviour merely by belonging to a creed founded in His name or by offering Him lip-praise. Only as we learn to shape our lives after the model of His own do we prove ourselves worthy of Him; and this can be done only by living His teachings. Jesus the Christ Himself taught this lesson to His disciples,

when He said to them: "And why call ye
me, Lord, Lord, and do not the things
which I say? Every one that cometh unto me, and heareth my words, and doeth
them, I will show you to whom he is like:
he is like a man building a house, who
digged and went deep and laid a foundation upon the rock: and when a flood
arose, the stream broke against the house
and could not shake it; because it had
been well builded. But he that heareth,
and doeth not, is like a man that built a
house upon the earth without a foundation; against which the stream brake, and
straightway it fell in; and the ruin of that
house was great."

If we wish to be saved we must connect
ourselves with the source of salvation. We
may have a hidden treasure, but we must
be conscious of it; otherwise we suffer
from poverty. Similarly, unless we know
our connection with the Infinite Ocean of

life and wisdom, we cannot be saved by It. That is the real significance of the idea that Christ takes the burden of those who come to Him. Why does He not take the burden of all? Because all do not bring their burden to Him. The majority of us rely on our ego, not on Him. But so long as we depend on that which is perishable and limited, we shall never attain to that which is imperishable and lasting. Saviours have come and gone, yet how many souls have failed to recognize them! This shows that we cannot be saved until we have unfolded certain spiritual qualities within ourselves. Man has been given frequent opportunities to save himself. He has been blessed countless times by God and by great Teachers; but he has not been able to profit by them because his mind is under the sway of ego.

Unless the mind is ready, even though a Saviour may come He can do little for

us. It is the mind which causes all our
unrest and it is the mind which makes us
calm and serene; it is this mind which
makes us happy and this very same mind
can make us miserable. We should take
care of this mind, therefore, because it is
the determining factor in all our under-
takings. Upon it alone rests our success
or failure. No one can say then that our
destiny depends on anything outside ourselves. For this reason Sri Krishna declares in the Bhagavad-Gita: "Let a man
raise himself by his higher Self, let him
never lower himself; for he alone is the
friend of himself and he alone is the enemy
of himself. He who has conquered himself by his higher Self, he is the friend of
himself; but he whose self is unconquered,
his self acts as his own enemy, like an external foe." The idea, therefore, that if
we believe in a certain Saviour we have
only to fold our hands and let Him save

us, is a grave mistake. Unless we lead a true life and uplift ourselves, even a Saviour cannot bring us salvation.

It is only through our life that we can prove the truth of a Saviour's message. We must not only hear His words, but assimilate them; and assimilation requires practice, leading an inner spiritual life. Christ declared that not those who merely cry, "Lord! Lord!" will enter the Kingdom of Heaven, but those who do God's will. Buddha taught His disciples never to try to convert by words, but by holy acts; because He knew that the only true help lies in converting a man's soul to righteousness, not merely in changing his faith from one form to another. Living the life is what every Saviour preaches; infilling each thought, deed and word with spiritual power. Spirituality is a living force. When we allow ourselves to be wholly guided by this force, resisting all lower impulses, we make ourselves ready for the Lord's saving grace. The mirror of our heart must be washed clean by the practice of forbearance, charity and loving-kindness towards all, then it will be able to reflect the image of our Saviour.

Those who are unworthy have not the spiritual sight necessary to perceive a Saviour. Who is to know when God comes? Only those who are God-like, whose vision is clear. We must first prepare the field. We must have a real thirst for righteousness in our hearts. We must feel as Buddha felt,—that this whole world is a vast prison house, that life is not safe without Truth. Although surrounded by luxury and living in conditions which mortals most long for, He saw misery and death haunting Him at every step and He felt He must save His fellowmen from these. To do it He plunged within Himself; He fixed His whole heart in His inner being, and that gave Him the power to discover the remedy for all mortal ills.

The true Saviour is within us. As soon as we analyze and turn our thought inward, we discover that the kingdom of heaven is an inner spiritual state, not an external realm of enjoyment. Merely believing that some one from the outside can save us is not sufficient. Ignorance is the cause of our bondage; rising out of ignorance is our salvation. In accomplishing this, the personal example and inspiration of a Saviour or divinely-appointed Teacher is of incalculable help. We must, however, establish a close relation with Him; we must listen to His voice and obey His teachings. Simply declaring ourselves His followers with fanatical devotion will not open us to His saving grace. We must mould our life in the smallest detail according to His injunctions; we must constantly bear in mind that the saving power of religion does not lie in a superficial acceptance of the form, but in holy living. We must base our daily actions on the fundamental principles of every religion,—humility, purity and love. We must give up all hypocrisy and half-heartedness. We must be absolutely sincere and steadfast in our spiritual devotion.

The Vedic Scriptures teach that it does not matter what personal Saviour we follow. If in our daily living we practice the teachings of any great Teacher, we shall surely realize the One who is the basic rock of all. The idea of a Saviour cannot be limited to one form or to one conception of Divinity. According to Vedanta, God comes to earth whenever there is a need; and He comes to all men, not to one special group of people. His form is universal. He is the Infinite Father of all, but He appears to His children in many different garments. When we lack direct perception of Truth, we see differences and sow seeds of discord; but the more we grow in inner wisdom, the more we shall learn to tolerate all creeds and see the same God in all Saviours and all religions.

VII
CHRISTIANITY AND VEDANTA

Christianity, as it is known and accepted, is based on the life and teachings of Jesus the Christ. Vedanta is not founded on the life of any personality. Christianity is about 2000 years old, while Vedanta has been in existence for 4000 years and maybe longer. When we study these two without any prejudice or bias, we find that, apart from all secondary considerations of time, climate and conditions, they represent unity of Truth — and Truth is eternal. He whom we regard as the all-merciful Father has never been absent from his creation since its beginning (if there ever was a beginning) and has always loved his children. Therefore we must study religion and philosophy not from a sectarian point of view, not with any dogmatic idea, but with a broad, sympathetic and earnest desire to know the Truth for the sake of itself, and not merely to satisfy our own preconceived ideas and notions.

Christianity has been recognized as a religion for only about 1600 years, yet there have been zealous, devout ministers of the gospel, who in their eagerness to convert the whole world to the Christian faith, taught that no unconverted people could attain salvation or know true freedom or perfection. But if merely being converted to Christianity is all that man needs to insure his peace and liberation, then why all the unrest and confusion in the world? Does it not show us beyond any doubt that the purpose of any religion is something far greater than conversion? I firmly believe that Christ never taught dogma, for as we study the New Testament we find him striving against the existing religious restrictions. Actually he brought a new interpretation of the old Hebraic faith. He did not come to destroy, but to bring purification and a newer, fresher understanding, so that people would no longer cling to the nonessentials, and fight for them, and base their faith upon them.

That was indeed the message of Christ, but as time rolled on, those who considered themselves Christian, who identified themselves with the "church" or, in other words, with what we know as organized Christianity, forgot the very purpose for which Christ incarnated, and began to preach their religion with fanatic fervor. Unfortunately, this course brought about a certain degradation of the original idea because you cannot force religion on people. No one can enforce his own particular belief upon another mind. The minute we try to do so we arouse antagonism.

In India the holy men also preached their religion because there was an ancient, organized religion of the Vedas, but there was no attempt at imposing their point of view upon anyone. We find an illustration of this Indian attitude in Asoka, the great Buddhist king who, about the year 250 B.C. sent missionaries to all parts of the world, and had erected in India stone tablets on one of which was inscribed the following:

"In truth, the King, dear to the gods, has at heart security for all creatures, respect for life, peace and happiness. These are the things that the King, dear to the gods, takes to be the conquests of religion."

The ideal of love of Divine fatherhood with all mankind as children of that Father did not originate with Christ, but was known among the Greeks and among other peoples who were true worshippers of God.

In fact what Christ taught—freedom in Truth, freedom of the individual, freedom from dependence on ritual and dogma in order that the real spirit of religion might be revealed through the life—was very like the

Indo-Aryan teaching. To those who really see below the surface, the teachings of Christ and those which we find recorded in the Vedas are one and the same. In fact one explains the other, that is, for the person who can approach an old faith without prejudice, without shrinking away because it bears a strange or unusual name.

We must not forget that Christianity was Oriental and that Christ's message was not alien to spiritual ideals already in existence. He came to fulfil; but unless we know what he came to fulfil, it will be very difficult for us to do justice to his message. All the great religions proclaim certain fundamental principles, such as non-killing, nonstealing and love for every living thing. These commandments you will find not only in the Old and New Testaments, but in all the bibles of the world.

When a man asked Jesus what was the greatest commandment, he said: "Thou shalt love the Lord thy God with all thy heart, and with all thy soul and with all thy mind. This is the first and great commandment. And the second is like unto it: Thou shalt love thy neighbor as thyself."

To me these two sayings contain the whole secret of spiritual living, for the first commandment seeks to awaken in man that love for God which leads to realization of his oneness with God, without which he can never fulfil the second commandment—to love his neighbor as himself. For only as man finds his relationship with the One will he know his relationship with the many. These two commandments given by Christ are universal and eternal.

Wherein then lies the difference between Christianity with its gospel of love and forgiveness and, say, Vedanta with its all-inclusive vision, or Buddhism which lays tremendous emphasis on the same great principles? The organized church which seeks to enlarge its scope through preaching and pro-

selytizing strikes a wrong note. For religion is
not a mere conversion from one faith to
another, but a conversion of the soul to
Truth. Buddhist missionaries understood that,
and Vedanta proclaims that we should not
assert our own ideas in a spirit of denunciation. God is infinite, He is One without a
second, but He is seen differently by His
various children, and is called by .different
names according to their comprehension.

It is through the life that we prove that a
message is true. Therein is the sum and
substance of all religion. For when we live the
life, when we follow the road of genuine
righteousness, we are bound to reach the
point where all spiritual paths converge. If we
are not willing to do that, if we see only
differences and seek to elevate our own faith
by tearing down the faith of others, then
there can be only quarrel and bloodshed. And
what religion upholds such things? No one
will say that his Bible, his Saviour would

allow him to do wrong to anyone whether belonging to his own faith or to another.

We can see that unless man's heart is enlightened by the love of God, it will be impossible for him to follow the second great commandment which tells us to love all and hate none. How can we realize brotherhood, the oneness of all souls, if we are ignorant of the very first principle on which our life is based, that is, Godhead? Christianity proclaims that we should learn to love God. This is also the first and foremost doctrine of every great religious system. Nonlove for any creature cannot be a part of any true spiritual teaching. Why then is there so much hatred in the world, such denunciation, especially among people who profess the same religion? It makes us doubt whether men have really adopted the spiritual message of their various faiths.

Christianity must explain one thing. If it is based on the life, character and gospel of the

gentle, noble and all-loving Jesus of Nazareth,
then from where comes the present form of
cruel and destructive intolerance which has
given rise to most terrible wars? We know that
Christ has no part in it and that sectarianism
has little to do with the true spirit of
Christianity or any religion. Christianity, as it
originated with Jesus, can be applied in the
Orient as well as in the Occident, for it bears
the mark of the Eternal, of Truth, forgiveness
and love. The same thing we can say of the
religious ideals which existed among the
Indo-Aryans from time immemorial. They
carried the identical message, although perhaps expressed differently.

When we do not grasp the keynote of
religion and of life, then out of our misunder-
standing we fight and quarrel and forget our
common origin and that we are all created in
the image of God and are related to Him. We
find that this is especially true amidst the
clamor of modern civilization. Religion has

gone out of fashion. To love God with one's whole heart seems ridiculous to some people, while praying openly is often looked upon as almost an ignorant act. We have been too much absorbed with material ideas. We have gone too far away from Godhood. Unless we can revive our spiritual ideals, not only in relation to our religious life, but in every aspect of our living, no matter how much we may try to build for happiness, the result can only be misery because we will not have built upon the right foundations. The right foundations require that we dig deep into the meaning of the scriptures in order to discover the essential nature of the great saviours of the world.

These saviours do not come from one race or from one group of people, but they speak the same spiritual language and pronounce the same Truth. The Vedanta scriptures state that they come in order to regenerate religious ideals and to show man the path leading toward God. The Lord Sri Krishna proclaims in the Gita:

"O Bharata, whenever there is decline of virtue and predominance of vice, then I embody Myself. For the protection of the good and for the destruction of evil-doers and for the reestablishment of virtue and religion I am born from age to age."

According to the Vedanta concept there is no one manifestation known as the Saviour of mankind; there are many manifestations of the one Supreme, Creative Power—the One Lord, who out of compassion, out of love for His children comes to lead them Godward. Therefore there can be no contradiction in the teachings which are given, for they all bear the same stamp of authority. They all bring the same infinite-Truth. They bring the spirit of unity and not that of destruction.

Now this we do not understand when in taking up one form of religion, we refuse to study any other. It is good to have faith, it is good to have love for our ideal, but our love and faith must not be fanatical. Sometimes we make our God so limited that He even falls short of our standard for the ideal man. Therefore we must expand our vision and create for ourselves a concept of divinity that is not narrow and limited, but all-inclusive.

Take Jesus the Christ, for instance. In order to grasp his true nature and magnitude we must cease to limit him to one particular time and place, but see him in relation to the teachers who came before him, and not hold the attitude that the peoples of the earth who existed prior to his birth were for that reason doomed to perdition. To think that those who believe in the dogmatic doctrine of the Christian church are saved while all others are lost, is a very limited belief indeed.

Personality is not all of religion, and whenever we try to assert one personality over all others, it is bound to create antagonism and cause disaster. The Vedanta philosophy, as I have said, is not based on personality. The same Truth which Lord Krishna interpreted and which Buddha, the Compassionate One, expressed through his illumined life has always existed, for It is eternal just as God and creation are eternal. It never began with one personality or at any one time. Those who hold this belief are always inclusive and not exclusive in their spiritual outlook. It is the reason why Vedanta does not seek to proselytize, and is never in conflict with any other religious faith.

When one has been brought up under orthodox influences, this universal attitude may be difficult to understand. In orthodoxy you accept one belief and denounce all others. Often I have heard people ask: "How can you tolerate so many contradictory ideas?" We forget that our inability to accept certain concepts may be due to our own limitations. There may come a time when these "contradictory ideas" may be-

come a part of our consciousness. Spiritual
growth is a matter of assimilation. But assimilation requires that we become imbued with
our ideals through applying them in our daily
life instead of merely dwelling on the ex-
ternals of religion. As Christ said to his
disciples:

"Not every one that saith unto me, Lord,
Lord, shall enter into the kingdom of heaven;
but he that doeth the will of my Father which
is in heaven."

Lord Buddha made somewhat the same
pronouncement when he declared: "He who
does not do what I command, sees me in vain.
This brings no profit. Whilst he who lives far
off from where I am, and yet walks right-
eously is ever near me. A man may dwell
beside me, and yet, being disobedient, be far
away from me; while he who obeys the Law
will always enjoy the bliss of the Buddha's
presence."

The Buddhist missionaries were wonderful

illustrations of this living aspect of religion. Wherever they went they practised nonkilling, nonstealing, forgiveness even of their enemies, not even recognizing any enemies. Through these means they converted the souls of people and not merely sought to change them from one outer form of faith to another.

Spirituality is a living thing. When it touches us, inspires us, then we begin to see things as they are in reality, but until then we doubt and quarrel and cannot help but antagonize. To live the life of the spirit in every act, every word and throughout every moment of one's existence — this is what Vedanta stands for. When you can live the Christ ideal, then you may be called a Christian, and when people of other faiths live according to their own bibles and saviours, then alone will they prove themselves true disciples of their masters, true examples of the religion which they profess. When we can all forget our differences in this way, then we shall become united. Through love we shall realize peace and come to know that we are all brothers.

There is a story told of a man who became lost in the wilderness. Night was falling and there was a heavy mist over everything which completely hid his path. As he peered into the gathering darkness he perceived a form approaching, and at once he was overcome by fear. He thought that it was a large animal seeking to destroy him. But as the form drew nearer he saw it was not an animal but a man, and his frightened mind told him it was a robber who would surely steal the little he had and kill him in the bargain. He knew not where to run, so he stood still and suddenly as he watched the stranger approach he realized he was no stranger but his own brother.

So it is often with us. We view things through the mist of ignorance and great distance, and we fear. Take the name Vedanta, for instance. Because it is strange to

us and represents an ancient philosophy or
faith, we feel that it is alien, that we must not
go near it, or it will lead us astray. When,
however, we approach it as we study it and
other ancient religions with unbiased minds,
with a real desire to know the truth, we find
that not only does it not harm us, it enlarges
our concept of truth, and actually throws
light upon our own religion and helps us to
understand it better. The meaning of Christ's
teaching is sometimes hidden, but it is illumined in the light of teachings that went
before. Christ himself could not fulfit the
revelations of the past unless he included
them in his life and gospel.

What is the significance of religion? Religion points the way to God. Religion shows
our relationship to the Infinite and cannot be
divided. Can we divide the infinite sky? Can
the infinite Godhead be divided? That One is
open to all living beings, and when It expres-

ses through our life we abandon all narrowness.

Since this universal concept forms the basis of Vedanta, Vedanta stands for the ideal of tolerance. It holds that even when we do not understand a new or an ancient idea or its expression of Deity, we have no right to condemn it; rather our duty is to show sympathy and a tolerant spirit. In India there was a great soul who often said to his disciples: "When you cannot love another, when you cannot see the beauty of an ideal coming from another source, do not denounce it. Allow to those who follow it the same privilege that you yourselves desire, then you will never strike a discordant note." Did Christ ever teach any of his followers to attack those who did not agree with him? Did he not, as he hung upon the cross, willingly forgive his enemies? If we profess to follow the life of such a teacher and then take the opposite course, it is a mockery.

What the world needs is the living example. Where people become illumined through living the principles of their religion, they bring a benediction to all mankind. The great truth of the divine Reality in the soul of man can only be taught by manifesting It. Only as we learn truly to love the Lord our God, shall we be able to realize our oneness with our brother.

Thus it is that we find no vital differences between the Christian bible and the ancient scriptures handed down to us from time immemorial. Let us learn to love God, realize Him and find in Him our whole inspiration and strength. Doing this we shall become fitting instruments for good in the world. But first we must acquire the gift of understanding by means of surrender to the Lord abiding in the hearts of all, that through openness of heart we may know, we may realize the oneness of that infinite Being.

The ancient rishis of India having attained

that goal, proclaimed in undying voice for all time:

God is One, Truth is One without a second, but we His children worship Him differently and call Him by different names.

PART II

Selections of Oriental Ideals

"There is hardly one religion which does not contain some important truth,—truth sufficient to enable those who seek the Lord, and feel after Him, to find Him in their hour of need."
—Max Müller.

I

SUPREME DEITY

HE is the Eternal among eternals, the Thinker among thinkers, who, though one, fulfills the desires of many. The sun does not shine there, nor the moon and stars, nor these lightnings and much less this fire. When He shines, everything shines after Him; by His light all this is lighted.

He makes all, He knows all, the Self-caused, the Knower, the Time of time; who assumes qualities and knows everything; the Master of nature and of man.

Only when men shall roll up the sky like a hide will there be an end of misery, unless God has first been known.—*Svetasvatara-Upanishad*.

The Blessed Lord said: I am the Father of the universe, the Mother, the Sustainer. . . . I am the Way, the Supporter, the Lord, the Witness, the Abode, the Refuge, the Friend, the Origin. . . .

Arjuna said: O boundless Form, Thou art the Primeval Deity, the Ancient Being, Thou art the Supreme Refuge of this universe; Thou art the Knower, the One to be known and the Supreme Abode. By Thee alone is this universe pervaded. . . . Salutations to Thee, my salutations a thousand times, again and again my salutations to Thee. Salutations to Thee before, salutations to Thee behind, salutations to Thee on all sides! O All, infinite in power and immeasurable in valor, Thou pervadest all, therefore Thou art all.

—*Bhagavad-Gita.*

This Word is indeed *Brahman* (the Absolute). This Word is indeed the Supreme.

He who knows this Word obtains whatever he desires. This is the best Support; This is the highest Support; he who knows this Support is glorified in the world of *Brahman.—Katha-Upanishad.*

In the beginning was the Word, and the Word was with God, and the Word was God.—*St. John.*

II

DEVOTION AND SURRENDER
TO GOD

FILL thy heart with Me, be thou devoted to Me, do thou worship Me and bow down to Me. Thus thou shalt attain unto Me. Truly I promise thee, for thou art dear to Me. Giving up all *Dharmas* (righteous and unrighteous actions) come unto Me alone for refuge. I shall free thee from all sins; grieve not.

—Bhagavad-Gita

Come unto Me, all ye that labor and are heavy laden, and I will give you rest. Take my yoke upon you and learn of Me; for I am meek and lowly in heart: and ye shall find rest unto your souls.—*Jesus the Christ.*

Man may rest in the eternal fitness; he may abide in the everlasting. . . He may bring his nature to a condition of One; he may nourish his strength; he may harmonize his virtue, and so put himself into partnership with God.—*Chuang Tzu.*

Mother, my Divine Mother, I am the machine, Thou art the one who runs the machine; I am the room, Thou art the tenant; I am the sheath, Thou art the sword; I am the chariot, Thou art the charioteer; I do whatever Thou makest me to do; I speak as Thou makest me to speak; I behave as Thou makest me to behave. Not I, not I, but Thou, but Thou.
—*Sri Ramakrishna.*

Source of my life, like unto Whom there can be nothing; Who alone canst fulfill the desires of Thy faithful ones; O Friend of the helpless, Shelter of the homeless, having no other refuge, I take refuge in

Thee. Grant unto me supreme devotion, supreme knowledge and supremest love. And through these may I come to know Thine Eternal Being. Make me Thy servant, finding sole delight in Thy divine command. Make me Thine own, lost forever in absorbing love for Thee.

—*Sri Ramanuja.*

A wise and good man submits to Him who administers the whole, as good citizens do to the laws of the commonwealth. This is the way that leads to freedom, this is the only deliverance from slavery, to be able at length to say from the bottom of one's soul: "Conduct me, Jove, and thou, O Destiny, wherever your decrees have fixed my lot. I follow cheerfully, and did I not, wicked and wretched, I must follow still."—*Epictetus.*

God has not made man with two hearts within him. The Incomparable Majesty who has conferred the boon of existence upon thee, has placed within thee but one heart, to the end that with a single heart thou mayest love Him alone and mayest turn thy back on all besides and devote thyself to Him alone, and refrain from dividing thy heart into a hundred portions, each portion devoted to a different object.

—Jami.

Thou art the Supreme Lord; Thou canst be approached by Thy worshippers only through whole-hearted devotion. Thou art the Primal Cause of the universe, its Protector and Transformer. O All-beautiful One, Refuge of the world! I am powerless, without friends or shelter; I know no guide other than Thyself. Take me under Thy care and protection and save me from the afflictions of the world.

—Mahabharata.

When all thoughts, all words and all deeds are given up unto the Lord, and the

least forgetfulness of God makes one in-
tensely miserable, then love has begun.
—*Narada.*

Dost thou of a truth desire Him the Hid-
    den to discover?
Then go look for Him, O seeker, with the
    longing of a lover;
Go not groping in the dark with learning's
    horny lantern dim,
Borrow eyes of those who love Him; thus,
    O seeker, look for Him.
—*Jalaluddin Rumi.*

Be bold as a leopard, light as an eagle,
swift as a roe, and strong as a lion, to do
the will of thy Father who is in Heaven.
—*Talmud.*

III

LOVE OF MAN

HE who hates no creature and is friendly and compassionate to all, who is free from attachment and egotism, equalminded in pleasure and pain, and forgiving; who is ever content and meditative, self-subjugated and possessed with firm conviction, with mind and intellect dedicated to Me, he who is thus devoted to Me is dear to me.—*Teaching of Sri Krishna.*

Love your enemies, bless them that curse you, do good to them that hate you, and pray for them that despitefully use you, and persecute you; that ye may be the children of your Father which is in Heaven. . . Do unto others what ye would have others do unto you.—*Teaching of Jesus the Christ.*

You must so adjust your heart that you long for the welfare of all beings, including the happiness of your enemies. If a man foolishly does me wrong, I will return to him the protection of my ungrudging love; the more evil comes from him, the more good shall go from me. . . Let us live happily then, not hating those who hate us. Among men who hate us let us dwell free from hatred. . . With pure thoughts and fullness of love, I will do towards others what I do for myself.

—*Buddha*.

When a person abstains from doing wrong to any creature, in thought, word, or deed, he is said to attain to the state of oneness with God.—*Mahabharata*.

To the good I would be good. To the not-good I would also be good in order to make them good. Recompense injury with kindness. . . Of all noble qualities, loving compassion is the noblest.—*Laotze*.

We are all children of Heaven, and therefore should love one another, as Heaven loves us all.—*Kaibara Ekken, Japanese Sage*.

Next to faith in God, the chief duty of man is to treat his fellow-men with gentleness and courtesy.—*Arabian Wisdom*.

He who calleth the stricken and heavily-burdened his own is the man of God; truly the Lord must abide with him. He that taketh the unprotected to his heart and doeth to a servant the same kindness as to his own children is assuredly the image of God.—*Tuka-Ram, South Indian Saint*.

The good man loves all men. He loves to speak of the good of others. All within the four seas are his brothers. Love of man is the chief of all the virtues. . . The mean man sows, that himself or his friends may reap; but the love of the perfect man is universal.—*Confucius*.

Thou shalt not say, I will love the wise but I will hate the unwise. Thou shalt love all mankind.—*Talmud*.

IV

MEEKNESS AND FORBEARANCE

NOT to blame, not to strike, to live restrained under the law and to dwell on the highest thought, this is the teaching of the Awakened.—*Buddha*.

Put on armor that will harm no one, let thy coat of mail be that of understanding, and convert thine enemies to friends. Fight with valor, but with no weapon except the word of God.—*Guru Nanak*.

The wise man's freedom from grievance is because he will not regard grievances as such.—*Laotze*.

Love thy neighbor and suffer the little offences he may give you.—*Thales of Miletus*.

The virtuous follow this rule in life: when they suffer oppression, they display kindness. . . Forbearance is at first like poison, but when engrained in the nature it becomes like honey.—*Bustan of Sadi.*

To bear with those who revile us even as the earth bears up those who dig it is the first of virtues. Bear with reproach even when you can retaliate; but to forget it will be still better. Let a man by patience overcome those who through pride commit excesses. Those who endure abstinence from food are great, next to those who endure the uncourteous speech of others.

—*Tiruvalluvar.*

Those who worship the Merciful One are they who walk on the earth gently, and who, when fools speak to them, say "Peace."—*Koran.*

Harmlessness as the first flower, restraint of the wandering senses as a flower,

compassion for all beings as a flower, forbearance or forgiveness as a most special
flower, knowledge or wisdom unto salvation as a flower, penance or self-restraint
as a flower, meditation as a flower, and
truthfulness as a flower; these eight as
flowers shall prove acceptable to the Omni-
present.—*Prapanna Parijata.*

Blessed are the meek: for they shall
inherit the earth.—*Jesus the Christ.*

V

PURITY OF HEART

THE soiled mirror never reflects the rays of the sun, and the impure and unclean in heart who are subject to *Maya* (selfishness and ignorance) never perceive the glory of the Lord. But the pure in heart see the Lord as the clear mirror reflects the sun. Be holy, then.—*Sri Ramakrishna.*

Having realized Him by means of the highest religious practice with a pure mind and sincere heart, the wise will never meet with death. Hence the Sages declare that giving oneself wholly to the Lord is superior to all other forms of austerity.

—Taittirya-Upanishad.

Find God; purity, holiness, all else will come. Seek the Highest, always the Highest, for in the Highest is eternal bliss.

—*Swami Vivekananda.*

Make thyself an island; work hard, be wise! When thy impurities are blown away and thou art free from guilt, thou wilt not enter again into birth and decay. Let a wise man blow off the impurities of his soul, as a smith blows off the impurities of silver, one by one, little by little, and from time to time.

If we liberate our hearts from petty selfishness, wish no ill to others, and become clear as a crystal reflecting the light of truth, what a radiant picture will appear in us mirroring things as they are, without the admixture of burning desires, without the distortion of erroneous illusion, without the agitation of sinful unrest.

—*Buddha.*

Blessed are the pure in heart for they shall see God.—*Jesus the Christ.*

That happiness which belongs to a mind which by deep meditation has been washed clean from all impurity and has entered within the higher Self, cannot be described here by words; it can be felt by the inward power only. — *Maitrayana-Brahmana-Upanishad.*

Wherever in this world there are pure minds and pure hearts, the Lord is sure to reveal Himself; for He is Purity itself. Purity is His name: purity in those who listen, purity in those who preach. A longing for the Lord's message is sure to awaken where the heart is pure, where the mind is pure; and the power to satisfy this longing is sure to come where the heart is pure. Purity is, as it were, the Lord's vehicle; for where purity is, there the Lord has come.—*Swami Premananda, Disciple of Sri Ramakrishna.*

VI
UNITY AND TOLERANCE

H E is the one God, hidden in all beings, all-pervading, the self within all beings, watching over all works, dwelling in all beings, the witness, the perceiver, the only one, free from attributes.—*Svetasvatara-Upanishad*.

As one and the same substance, water, is called by different names by different peoples,—*eau, aqua, wasser, pani,* so the one *Satchidanandam* (Existence-Knowledge-Bliss Absolute) is invoked by some as God, by others as Allah, by still others as Jehovah, or as Divine Mother or *Brahman*.

Different creeds are but different paths by which to reach God. Many are the roads to the Temple of Divine Mother. Similarly, various are the ways to the house of the Lord. Every religion is such a path leading to the one Supreme Being.
—Sri Ramakrishna.

He that is praised is in fact only One. In this respect all religions are only one religion. Because all praises are directed towards God's Light, these various forms and figures are borrowed from it.
—Jalaluddin-Rumi.

The basis of all religions is the same, wherever they are; try to help them all you can, teach them all you can, but do not injure them.—*Instruction given Buddhist missionaries.*

Is God the God of the Jews only? Is He not the God of the nations also? Yea, of the nations also.—*St. Paul.*

Remain always strong and steadfast in thine own faith, but avoid bigotry and intolerance. Be not like the frog in the well, who knows nothing grander than its little well. So are all bigots; they do not see anything greater than their special creed. As you rest firmly on your own faith and opinion, allow others also the same liberty.—*Sri Ramakrishna*.

No decrying of other sects, no depreciation of others without cause, but on the contrary a rendering of honor to other sects for whatever cause honor is due. By so doing, one's own sect will be helped forward and other sects benefited; by acting otherwise, one's own sect will be destroyed in injuring others.—*Rock Inscriptions of Emperor Asoka*.

Brethren! Meet together, talk together, let your minds apprehend alike; common be your prayer; common be your purpose;

common be your desires; united be your
hearts; united be your intentions; so that
there may be a thorough union among you.
                                    —Rig-Veda.

VII
I ACCEPT ALL RELIGIONS

I accept all the religions that were in the past, and worship them all; I worship God with every one of them, in whatever form they worship Him. I shall go to the mosque of the Mohammedan; I shall take refuge in Buddha and his Law. I shall go into the forest and sit down in meditation with the Hindu, who is trying to see the Light which enlightens the hearts of everyone. Not only shall I do these things, but I shall keep my heart open for all that may come in the future.

If there is ever to be a Universal Religion, it must be one which will have no location in place or time; which will be infinite as the

God it will preach, and whose sun will shine upon the followers of Krishna and Christ, on saints and sinners, alike; which will not be Brahmanical or Buddhist, Christian or Mohammedan, but the sum total of all these, and still have infinite space for development; which in its catholicity will embrace in its infinite arms, and find a place for every human being, from the lowest grovelling savage, not far removed from the brute, to the highest man, towering by the virtues of his head and heart almost above humanity, making society stand in awe of him and doubt his human nature. It will be a religion which will have no place for persecution or intolerance in its polity, which will recognize divinity in every man and woman, and whose whole scope, whose whole force, will be centered in aiding humanity to realize its own true, divine nature.

Swami Vivekananda

Belief in one God is the corner-stone of all religions. But I do not foresee a time when there would be only one religion in practice. In theory, since there is one God, there can be only one religion. But in practice, no two persons I have known have had the same identical conception of God. Therefore, there will perhaps always be different religions answering to different temperaments and climatic conditions. — Mahatma Gandhi

The supreme critic on the errors of the past and the present, and the only prophet of that which must be, is that great nature in which we rest as the earth lies in the soft arms of the atmosphere, that unity, and that Oversoul within which every man's particular being is contained and made one with all other. Within man is the soul of the whole, the wise silence, the universal beauty, to which every part and particle is equally related, the eternal One.

—Ralph Waldo Emerson

CONCLUSION

What is the great object lesson we learn from these lofty sayings? That no one has a monopoly over truth. Fundamentally we are all one. There is no inherent difference between man and man or one ideal and another, but these differences are of our own making, fictitious and debasing; for what religious principle will ever uphold us in our hateful thoughts and cruel deeds? When we succeed in touching the inmost chord of our life, we can not help but strike a note of ineffable harmony.